· Exposure

· Broken Water Main

· Afterlife: Abandoned Mall

· Amelia Earhart, Rock Springs, 1931

· Soliloquy in the Old Nursery

· Mylar

· Keepsake

· Exodus with Lightly Sleeping Child

· Magi

· O Bird Singing or Whatever

· Fieldland Glory

· "Thunder has not harmed anyone we know"

· Afterlife: Formicarium

· Coliseum

Blueprint
and
Ruin

· Succession

· Outlook Hazy, Try Again

· Salvage

· The Birds Are Always in the Corn

· "Touch the mountain that it might smoke"

· Exile Queen

· Orchestra Playing as the Ship Goes Down

· Afterlife: Proving Grounds

· Afterlife: End of Tourist Season

· No Season for Figs

· "The executioner was very good"

· What Now Have You Been Eating

· Wildland-Urban Interface

· Cold Metal Cup

· Dear Highways of Our Nation, I Am Sorry

Also by Bethany Schultz Hurst

Miss Lost Nation

Blueprint and Ruin

Bethany Schultz Hurst

Winner of the 2021 Michael Waters Poetry Prize

Published by the University of Southern Indiana
Evansville, Indiana

ISBN 978-1-930508-52-1   First Edition

Printed in the USA

Library of Congress Control Number: 2022942006

This publication is made possible by the support of the Indiana Arts Commission, the National Endowment for the Arts, the University of Southern Indiana College of Liberal Arts, the USI English Department, the USI Foundation, and the USI Society for Arts & Humanities.

Southern Indiana Review Press
Orr Center #2009
University of Southern Indiana
8600 University Boulevard
Evansville, Indiana 47712

sir.press@usi.edu
usi.edu/sir
Ron Mitchell, Rosalie Moffett & Marcus Wicker, eds.

Cover art: *Pioneer*; © 2018 Laura Ahola-Young; *lauraaholayoung.com*
Cover design: Zach Weigand
Layout: Sarah Doan

Contents

One thing:

Tell me there is
A meadow, afterward.

–Lucie Brock-Broido

I

Exposure

Watch: the dog is first to go down
in the field.
                         The child

follows. Then the costumed lion, his soft
paws held up stiff

like a table flipped over. Then
snow begins to fall.

Stop.
        How I hover over

this timeline. Oh, but they'd almost made it
to the city. Their bodies sunk

into the flowers. When we

        trespassed across the fields
to the abandoned buildings

we too did not think
                         to wear protective masks

inside where we brushed past
the decaying insulation

        unsettling from the drywall
like an animal field-dressed.

                         Our matches

flicked and hissed. We lit
pilfered cigarettes. We were experts

        in searching our empty pockets

for our make-believe IDs, experts
in performing we'd left them

in our other grown-up coats.

Then back inside our houses
with our parents we became
children again.

Stop. How do those
small bad choices seem so huge

when disasters loomed large
around us

like shipyards, like the mines
where the owners kept

sending men down
into vermiculated tunnels

to extract their profit
from contaminated ore? Who

left behind sparkling fields

of slag in which the town's children
played and scrabbled, gasping

in the fibril dust. How we'll slip

anything shining into our pockets.
How we'll believe in

a glimmering city where we'll be given
anything we want.

But I could never get
my father to watch that movie

with me because he couldn't stand
its star. Or he couldn't

stand the smoky shell she became

once her producers prised her out.

                                        Stop.
In the flowering field
she is still a child.
                        Her eyelashes

are heavy with cinematic snow. Once

in college, half-lit, my roommate
and I together watched her open

an ordinary door
            to reveal a golden road

before her. We played that album
by Pink Floyd so that their stories
            intertwined.
                        Breathe.

Time. The Great Gig in the Sky.

We rewound and rewound to get back
            to the dark forest

where something was tangled
in the trees.
                        It was just a bird

unsettling its dark wing, but we preferred
the made-up explanation:

a stagehand, broken-necked
and broken-hearted, swinging
                        from a limb. We wanted

the awful rumor, not what was produced
for us to see. We'd learned

to be suspicious
of such slick beauty. In the crimson field

                    the child's eyelashes

are heavy
        with chrysotile snow.

The scarecrow flaps about, trying
to wake her, in his fireproof

clothes. Stop. I know now

those clothes were woven
from asbestos. I know now time

would eventually uncover

        what was already buried
in my roommate's haystack lungs.

But then, our fingers
                    hovered. Our faces

right up against the screen. Now

I replay the scenes to find
the needle hiding. When we descended

from exposed-asbestos attics
        in our mothers' outgrown

dresses, dust rising
from our shoulders. Stop. When

        we hopscotched over
our school's yellowed vinyl tiles. Stop.

When casually we parted thick plastic flaps
to reveal
        a dusty demolished wing.

Later behind a curtain

             in the hospital my roommate
breathed
                        into a machine. Ruby-speckled

tissue. Microscopic filaments
             hooked into her airways. Stop. I

didn't know

until she was gone. Stop. I never went
to see her. Stop. This part

                 is just a dream. I am there
with her and above us is always

a crumbling popcorn
          ceiling. In the field

thick drifts of it
                   are unmelting in the child's

hair. When she wakes,
          the city will shine before her.

Her beauty is a future

ruin. My father told me. Stop.
I watched without him and he retreated

to the rooms upstairs. How I hover

over a timeless field. When we left

the wrecked buildings behind us
          we clicked

our flashlights off, saw our own
gray houses.
                   Stop. We breathed in

the crystalline air.

We breathed out clouds.

We did not know
what was inside them. In the field

again we could not stop

the snow that had begun
to fall.

Amelia Earhart, Rock Springs, 1931

We're trying to leave the hotel, but keep forgetting
things back in the room: sunglasses, wallet,
paper cup full of coffee. I make multiple trips
from car to second story. The carpet is the same
in every hallway until I lose track of which floor
I'm on. I have to force myself to pay attention.
The car is running under the front awning.
The one insistence that we are somewhere specific
is the photographs in the halls: coal miners
below ground in 1928, a 1950s oil derrick
in "unknown location." Next to the check-in desk,
a framed photograph of Amelia Earhart
in a Rock Springs hangar where she'd stopped
to refuel. She's in front of her plane, smiling,
surrounded by locals who have turned out to see her.
One boy leans too far into the picture. It seems important
to remember this: her fabulous jumpsuit, the way
the propellers stretch out above her as if offering
some kind of shelter. When we finally leave,
we drive through blank desert country, tossing
our orange peels onto the car floor. We'll clean them
later. This feels like Western expanse. Stretches
of dirt, rock, sagebrush but punctuated by
pipeline stations and natural gas wells. Billboard:
*The most important thing to come out of our mines
is the miners.* They've tapped out on coal,
have moved onto trona, used as toothpaste filler
or to condition water or to clean the flesh
off trophy skulls. We probably have some
in our suitcases. Instead of town names, the exit signs
advertise chemical plants: Solvay, Tronox.
The names have changed since I last drove through.
We can't see it, but massive networks of mines
stretch beneath us. I'm already unable to recall
details of the hotel. We're driving toward a pile
of mist. I have trouble staying awake on this stretch.
In the past I've pulled over at abandoned gas stations
or firework stands to nap after scanning the radio
for station blips wore out. We're talking now

about my widowed sister, whom we agree
needs to move back home. She's still
living near the facility where her husband worked,
where they manufacture rocket motors,
where they store and treat hazardous waste. Wait,
that gorgeous white cloud on the horizon
is actually the Jim Bridger plant. Thirty-seven deaths
attributed annually to its fine particulate pollution.
It's called the Green River formation,
but everything here is brown, even the dog park
at Little America, which is just a gated plot
of dirt and concrete. My sister says she's afraid
she'll forget her husband's face if she leaves
their house. *That's what photographs are for,*
my husband says. But it's not the same. To have
to have a marker. We drive past the turnoff
for the fossil beds on cruise control. No one's sure
what caused the tumor. I scan the sky where
jet planes leave contrail messages I can't read.
A fraction of his cremains were launched into the air.
A crowd gathered. My sister was there to mark
the occasion and then the ceremony was over.
Ways we disappear into an expanse: clouds
look like islands and bodies become a cloud.
Magpies and crows congregate on smears
of roadkill every few miles. At first
I slow down when I spy each dark mass.
But if we're ever going make it home,
I have to trust their wings will stretch and
lift, that they'll scatter into the sky.

O Bird Singing or Whatever

o bird singing or whatever
it is you are doing
to endure this frigid cold

please stay inside that cage
of prickly juniper where

nothing wants to stick its hand
inside to crush you   o bird

forgive me for this news I bear
for this grim headline among
all others that I've chosen

to repeat but listen

sixty-four antelope
were hit by a train   and

what was once inside them
came spilling out   forgive me

for being gruesome I just want
someone to listen and also

while we're at it

forgive me for *forgive me*

for I have been trained
to say *I'm sorry*
when someone tells me

to not say that I am sorry
how many times
has it been confirmed

that my high-pitched voice

cannot be heard   not even Alexa
answers until I fake

a somber bass   so bird
what I am saying is

the antelope confirm for me
that beauty   I mean like

real beauty not like
false eyelashes

cannot be displayed cannot
go on snuffling

the snowy tracks for some secret
scent of earth

cannot expect to go on

not being hit by a train

and of course bird we both know
that I am talking

about you my own small

heart so dismissible and always
punctuated

like a question so forgive me for
being ridiculous? but I am

sometimes moved to tears
by the way you keep

fluttering in my chest I mean

I can't always hear it but some
song is surely spilling out

because your beak keeps on
chattering and chattering

like that

Broken Water Main

The utility crew's equipment beep-beeped
up our pitch-black cul-de-sac at 1, 2,
and 3 am. It was cold, and I felt bad

for the men working and worse for myself
as the jackhammer made our waterless house
shudder. I'd given up on trying to put down

the baby in her crib. In the dark,
I held her in one arm, open storybook
in the other. Foolish, I'd neglected

to fill jugs of water and worried now
what we'd do come morning. There are,
I admit, bigger problems: septic tanks

on this hillside leaking into the supply,
the entire country's aging pipes leaching
out copper, lead. This winter we're cautioned

against rivers swollen with melting snow
lest children slip in. The flood watch
never expires. Everything's washing

away. Last month we were surprised
by a massive water bill—my visiting dad
finally sleuthing a silently running toilet.

This is how I like a father: proving something huge
can be fixed with a brisk jiggle of a handle.
All the farmland this winter is under water,

but still a house on 3rd caught fire. Well,
of course: didn't I grow up reading about
babies floating down streams in baskets,

then bushes bursting into flame? My dad
changed all our burnt-out bulbs
while he was here. When she was alive,

he updated for my mother a spreadsheet
of her medications while she sat in
a comfortable chair and had good poison

dripped into her veins. She held a book
of devotions. What's to blame for all this
suffering? What can predict how much

awaits us down the road? The BPA
in canned peas and beans, the aspartame
in her sweet peach tea? The cornfields

of her childhood farm seem so serene
until you calculate how many million gallons
glyphosate were keeping them green. Didn't

I also grow up reading about babies about to be
cut in half, babies laid on altars instead of
in someone's arms? And these were the favorite

sons. The broken main wasn't our fault,
but the men flagged the soggy snow
in our front yard to chart the network

dripping underneath. They dug and dug
until they patched the problem. Now
morning breaks its cold light upon us. My

weary arms. I lay the baby down. Restored,
if just for the moment, water runs like prophecy
out from the faucet's mouth.

Keepsake

In the mornings my ex-boyfriend would excavate
his dreams, long and full of absurd details
of only personal significance, his eyes
shining in awe at what his brain unearthed
when he was not fully in control. He had
a nice smile but trouble holding down
a job. Even pushing grocery carts back
to their corrals became controversial
because he wouldn't stop smoking long enough
to do it with both hands. After a while I grew impatient
when he read aloud to me his novel pretty much
about himself but with a vaguely Italian name.
Why are my memories of him so mean?
Of that time I should recall the wildfire
out by the drive-in that exposed the mountain's
abandoned shafts. That it was someone's job
to fill them before clueless hikers tumbled in.
That on the other side of town sometimes cars
would crash when fog from the phosphate plant
hung too low. That birds taking off from the tailings pond
burst into flame when the dried phosphate
caught the wind. Did any of this
vein into his dreams? I don't know, I wasn't
listening. And somehow we didn't seem
alarmed. Look, there were distractions. He liked
good music and picked up litter. He had a jaw
like Ben Affleck. He'd maybe name a cat
Aaron Purr, if he had one. Now the drive-in
movie screen's been torn down,
but you can still see where the fire burned.
I sleep so hard when I'm allowed that I recall
only dark outlines of my dreams. My son
screams for me at night and I stagger in
to find his blankie, pull the covers to his chin.
Half-asleep, I can see approximately one
square inch of the mountain from my bedroom
window. A car's headlights flash as it hairpins
up the summit. And when I stumble into
sleep's opening, I tunnel in, headlamp flickering

on strata that's been mined before. I can't keep track
of the larger mountain, what's collapsed
or is a moment from catching flame. In the slurry
every job I've had that I was shitty at:
wrong drinks brought at intermission, gift wrap cut
an inch too short, the sales pitch that this
special-production Christmas ornament—formed
of polymers made from the sludge of ancient bodies,
then shaped into a fragile dove to hang upon
your tree—was really something special, something
that should become a memory, something
we should all like to keep.

Afterlife: Formicarium

You remember the mountain by hollowing it out.
Your past is arranged as if it belongs to a child—

those too-precious overalls, pale hair gleaming as the sun
streams out from behind a jagged peak. Even now

you cannot decide if you desire or despise a smooth
horizon. With a little yellow bulldozer one mound of dirt

is flattened to form another. The child is unaware of
the elaborate galleries below, unaware of the disturbed ants

troubling the ruffled boundary of her socks, but you
can see them dotting up her leg like instructions

to cut. You are arranging. A vivisected slice. Grain
after grain carried up from the mountain's dark

center. How you remember the shape of it,
when the skin on fire is no longer yours.

Mylar

The extra balloons nudge our ceiling, as if prodding
for a secret. Shiny golden stars trailing white ribbons.
The leftover birthday cake I am neither hiding nor

actively offering. When you pull out the candles
from the icing, they leave perfect circles like little
surgical scars. Each time I open the refrigerator door

I slice off a thin slab, inching closer and closer
to my son's red-piped name. In increments I've eaten
a dragon's tail, buttercream clouds, swaths

of black and purple sky. For the party, we'd crammed in
the cluster of balloons through the heavy arcade doors.
I watched one work free and give up to the wind,

a gold speck growing quickly smaller. A mistake I did not
point out. We know better now than to release them.
When I was a child we tied our addresses to the strings,

unafraid to declare our homes. Once I got a postcard
from a man in Texas who untangled from his fence
the busted-down balloon. Helium, like other

noble things, is mostly discovered by accident. Then,
nearly impossible to capture, it vanishes
into the air. I somehow did not realize the shortage,

helium's necessary medical use, until the arcade manager
told me how much we squander just for tricks,
just to diminish our voices, just to inflate these

foil pouches to bump stupidly around. I was still
holding the balloons. Before I could stop her
my little daughter wrapped a string around her fist, her

neck. She protested when I untied her as if she wanted
to be lifted somewhere else. Without "Happy Birthday,"
a name in red looks like an accusation. Or a warning.

Without helium, mylar is just those crinkly foil sheets
you see spread over children at the border, as if
they were leftovers someone keeps on poking through

to spoon out the best bits. When I drove to the party,
the balloons were a hazard, bobbing up behind me,
nudging up beside. The rearview mirror was filled

with their foolish dazzling light. When the party
was over, I pressed one into each child's palm
as if being gifted could make it necessary, could make it

a real star we could use to chart our course.

Magi

i

the nativity set is still packed away
in a storage tub I cannot find

and the tree   it's almost too big
for the room

what were we thinking

we don't have enough
to fill those empty branches

my brother-in-law in the hospital bed
did not know

who I was   and became

suddenly polite   like I were just
some stranger visiting

after the biopsy his head was shaved
and swaddled in bandages

for a while he and my sister
thought there would be a different ending

a miraculous surgeon
if they could travel far enough

to find him   there were holes

in his sentences backfilled with *I'm scared*

still he had an opinion
about what kind of mobile

I should buy my baby what colors
should spin above her in the dark

I got the one he said and feel

it is a gift now that he is gone

when I look up and all the birds
are tangled together

and they can't navigate either

still the baby points up at them
like a message

ii

I'd thought maybe I had lost it

but now wonder if I ever even bought
a tree topper   so now there's no finale

to lift our child up above the branches for

no moment to say *there now it's just right
now it's done*   when you look up

the lyrics to Little Drummer Boy

there's a whole lot of
pa rum pum pum pum

not much story there

but I guess that's the point
that just a melody can be a gift

my other brother-in-law
is still alive and has given us

the same lovely present two years
in a row   a bluebird night light

a reference to a song he likes
I hope he gives us

another one this year

I would like a whole flock

and on the top of the tree I would like
a star or angel but not if

they are going to be making any
more promises   wasn't there

supposed to be a hand that
stayed the knife

before it plunged into the beloved wasn't
there supposed to be

a reprieve   what are these angels doing

freaking everyone out and then telling them

not to be afraid   telling them
that a hole has opened in the sky

and heaven has poured in

iii

how do you go on
with the sheep etc

after that sort of news

when he fretted in the hospital bed
my sister soothed him

she was expecting

I tried to help   *what if I don't
live to see my girls* he said

shush I told him *of course you will*

and hoped at that moment
I was a stranger to him

with some good
tidings from a distant place

not his sister-in-law who would
say anything

to make it better

for my own baby this year
I bought a kaleidoscope

not thinking how she is too little
to hold it up to the light

too little to look through it
and discover all of those beautiful

stars that twist and shift
into other beautiful stars

that don't guide us
anywhere   but for a moment

take the place
of the empty sky

2

Coliseum

my mother forgave me

when I presented her
with the tulips

I'd dug up by the bulb

the excavators were already
clawing at the dirt

for our new house's foundation
so we wouldn't be

in this old house
next spring

to see the holes I'd made

in the ruined garden

⁋

after Mussolini exposed
the Coliseum
from its overgrowth

like a bone

Hitler ordered
that his own awful monuments

be built from stone so they too

would one day glisten
in their ruin

⁋

I wanted to be
dead and pretty too

when I grew up

floating down the river
past all the high houses

so everyone could see
my lovely

vacant face

⁓

years later

the walls of our new house
literally

dripped with honey

until the expert came
and pried the hive away

still golden light
seeped in our windows

even when the McMansion
sprang up next door

the light just poured
around it

⁓

when they unearthed
its ruinous sewer

the Coliseum flooded
for a while

into a little lake

whose stagnant water
was rife with fever

like a prayer you could
no longer understand

⸴

unable to be a whole tower

on the prairie broken
with quick-built houses

I practiced being

a shard of colored glass
you could press

into your palm and dream

of a cathedral

⸴

the next spring the bees
came back

their swarm took
the shape of a hive but

there was nothing inside
of all their murmuring only

their own innumerable bodies

⸴

what if I didn't have
to be either a monument

or a ruin I wondered

what if there could be an Earth
that we would never plow

but then how
would we live there

among all that unscythed grass
along what bank could we dwell

incandescent with our desire
to arrange it

⁊

before the Coliseum
was scoured clean
of its tangled garden

rare flowers grew there

from seeds shook out
from the honey-colored fur

of hungry lions as they paced

the trembling martyrs
who would not be saved

just remembered later
in the shape

of a dark cross

⁊

I dreamed I too drifted
a flooded plain

between the new-built houses

in the leaking vessel
my dress was

growing heavy and water
just kept on springing

from the hole

I looked toward the sky
for something to bail me out

but those weren't gothic spires
on the horizon

that was
the Purina Cat Chow factory

its many particulates
pluming the sky

⸺

what if ghosts
can only pour themselves

through whatever holes
have been worn through us

through whatever holes
we've bored into this world

⸺

and so I dreamed I let
the water fan my hair

into the shape
of a terrible mansion

into the idea
of a halo

into a thick-jewelled bloom
torn right out

of the ground

Exodus with Lightly Sleeping Child

My favorite pop stars are all dying now,
so I understand the desperate

bicyclists pumping into the night on
the shoulder's white line, only a miniscule

reflective flicker giving them away. Still, I curse
and hug the center. I miss how song lyrics

once could split my rocky heart open, turn me
into water. Prophetless, our next collective trick

is to vanish into dust. At the dangerous corner,
a handful of makeshift crosses decked out

in plastic flowers poke out of the weeds.
I can't read their markered names from here. I'm

just driving and driving, afraid to go home
where the baby will surely wake when the car

stops jiggling under her. I've already wandered
through the Old Testament subdivision

where my father-in-law lives: turn right
on Eve, and Moses is a cul-de-sac,

Moses, whose first home—like all of ours—
was a watery womb before he was set afloat

in a basket made of reeds. No wonder
the staff became a snake when he threw it

from his grasp. No wonder my husband mistakes
the good hand towels for bathmats. We can't keep

anything nice. We've got to keep moving. A little north
of here is a house built atop a winter den for snakes.

Each disbelieving new owner signs a disclosure
not understanding what it means to hear scales

sliding through the siding or to broom away the snakes
each morning before the children wake. Already

milk is weeping from my body's walls. Have you
ever been to a hilltop and considered the vista

of beautiful homes, knowing you will never
settle there? I'm always driving through

the desert on the interstate's black river. The radio
broadcasts an empty hiss. There is no street name

for where we're going. I'm afraid
I hear a slither in the tire walls. How it must feel

to be picked up out of the weeds, to be held
as son or daughter, to wake up at last

inside the palace after a whole life of moving
from one strange house into the next.

Afterlife: Abandoned Mall

through broken skylights
the sun
      chiaroscuros

into the empty food court into

the Sbarro's we recognize though
its letters have been taken

from the wall

      we have enough past now

that even it can be wrecked   O

incomplete mannequin,
you never did have more
than a suggestion

for a face   now ruin
has made you extraordinary

stripped you of your golden
belts   relieved you of your

full-price scarves and leather purses

      unarranged

you from your pedestal   and still

you are displayed   which

        motionless escalator
    ascends into
the greater darkness

of the ceiling's missing

pieces   blackened eyes
or teeth   just let us

recognize a face or even
a hand stretching out
           into this disaster

     for what we save
becomes at last

somehow ours   O past

we were missing from you
passing by your glass storefronts

arms weighed down by awkward
     clearance

      restore us to this

empty fountain   the potted tree
the ashtray   the glass

     elevator junked out

where once we could rise and
see through our blurred

     reflection

where once we could rise
     and believe

that we were seen

Soliloquy in the Old Nursery

Spotlit in the window, I pick burrs out
from the gossamer of my nightgown.

If by *gossamer* I can mean affordable
polyester blend. Across what moors

have I been roaming? Always I wished
for a tunic made of skeleton leaves

to billow and silhouette around me
when I'm on the darkened sill again,

ready to be led straight into morning.
And how long have I been waiting? I should

be old enough now to get it. To know
that no one's coming. Look, don't look

at me in this revealing light. I never
wore a bikini. Swimming pools only

interest me if they are drained
and/or full of leaves. We passed

the abandoned water park on the way
to a funeral last week and even from

the road I could hear the familiar clock
the crocodile swallowed. So what if

I never loved my shadow. I don't even
have to check to know that it's there

behind me, fool in a velvet robe dragging
tattered through the weeds. I know now

we shall come no more to the lost malls
of my youth, will never sow another coin

into their over-chlorinated fountains. Never
circle through their tiers in my tightest

worn-out jeans. *Never, never, never,*
never, never, said the king. I am permitted

no more into that childish kingdom
and have no other to bequeath. Of course

the malls were built on landfills, of course
they were named for fairy tales and

their shifting foundations gave way.
What comfort did I think could be

unearthed from that great decay? And
tell me, have I been in my nightgown

throughout this entire play? Pray you,
undo this button. I am done with all

this fooling. My heart made faster
by every flutter in the drapes. Go on

and blow, winds: one day it will be
my children who will vanish

through that window whether or not
I've left a kingdom. When they return

I'll be the child who replaced them,
wavering in my unsteady throne,

waiting for someone to wrap
around me the seedy bedclothes

that have fallen to the floor.

Field and Glory

First this country was an infant. Then it cut its teeth
on anything it could fit into its mouth. Can we pretend
that it's a protest, not watching its fireworks up close?
This morning we were at the fairgrounds, though, in line

with giant slushies, paying to paint the children's faces
into whiskered cats. Now we've retreated to the hillside
by the potato field with the view we thought was secret

until a series of arriving cars spit out gravel in the mud.
Out climb teenage girls, all poofed hair and prairie dresses,
like someone's fantasy pioneer. You'll see them
sometimes, the polygamists, skirting in from the edge

of town. Some man has imagined such plenty to be
ordained. Imagined his seed should be as innumerable
as the stars. They've come here to see the spectacle

without being spectacles themselves, the way
they grocery shop late at night when the aisles are empty
but for their listing carts. I've seen them, trailing
children, interrupting the stocked shelves' easy promise

of anything we could want. On the dark hill,
parked machinery looms behind us. In the waning light
my daughter's face is a confusing smudge, but

she's not done imagining she's an animal. You could
pretend this newborn road was carved just so we could see
the valley spilling out before us. But the excavator
will keep at the dirt until the field gives way

to a thousand costly homes. I keep trying to better see
the girls, who have spread out into the field, bowing
now and then to press their faces to the crops

as if they'd wandered into some fragrant garden
instead of sprayed and irrigated rows. My daughter
is at first uneasy when the city bursts at last into smoke
and glimmer. We lose sight of anything but sky. We pretend

the bursting lights are fountains, fast-blooming roses,
collapsing domes of huge cathedrals. Full skirts
we could wear or sprawl beneath. Who wouldn't want

to lie beneath a flamboyant tree and be carried skyward
by its blossoms. To see a seed festoon its ridiculous beauty
across the dark field of sky. To watch with open mouths
as the starry darkness is devoured.

Blueprint and Ruin

When we moved with our first newborn
into this '70s raised ranch house,
I pretended some benevolent ghost
could soothe him. Clearly, even someone
dead could be a better mother. I paced
the wailing baby, envisioning a different
place. Busted out some doorways. Imagined
the popcorn ceiling scraped. I was
convinced under the shag carpeting
I could hear some hardwood creak.
I was still freaked out about holding
something human that felt so thoroughly
untame. In high school I liked being
afraid, snuck into the old pioneer houses
outside of town or the mid-century A-frame
languishing on the market, where one night
my friend ditched her weed in the half-broke
kitchen drawer when the cops showed up
and we ran. We had to go back the next day
in cold daylight to retrieve it. Well, we didn't
have to, but it felt like it then. It was scarier
in sunlight when anyone might see us
slinking in. Those razed houses are now
a rehab center, sprawling outdoor mall—
exact location maybe PF Chang's or
Lowes? And here I am in Aisle 12 considering
cabinet pulls and maybe someone's foot
is buried beneath. Once I was a girl who loved
a skeleton, who wanted to see a body
down to its bones, to see into the next room
through the hole punched in the first.
To swallow something whole, then spit out
its seeds. To answer to no one. Or maybe
to answer to a different name, like *Persephone*—
that lucky girl was wild because at any moment
she could go back home, find her mother waiting
there. In flipped houses on tv, ripped out walls
always equal added value. But that's not really
what I'm after. I'm pissed off my wardrobes

never open up like portals no matter what
new hardware I install. Where's the ghost
who can replace my mother? If only I were
a house. Then wreck me—whosoever, either
architect or vandal—bust these useless walls
and let in the ragged morning light.

"Thunder has not harmed anyone we know"

I dreamed lightning struck and toppled
the huge ponderosa pine beside
my father's house. I have to say
my father's house now because

my mother is gone. The moment
it takes me to make that edit is at once
unnoticeable and unfathomable
like a canyon you can't see in an open field

until you stand right at its rim. It feels
somehow like a hymn. Like a choir whose
song has fallen behind the organ's march.
The tree's giant body fell the only way

it could without smashing the house.
We were so lucky. Would we see more
of the mountains now, or just the sprawling
house next door? How my mother once

mourned its building, the ridiculous pitch
of its roof smack dab in the middle
of our picture view. I pitied the dumb
house that had mistook its ceiling

for a cathedral's. How many devotions
have we mistaken for prayer? In my dream
the thunder echoed. When I woke I still
could hear it, couldn't believe it could be

confined inside a dream. In a moment
it would be muted, the dream-felled tree
would be righted, and then I'd be
standing again in the morning

where I'd lost an entire forest.

3

Exile Queen

the trees
      flaunting their flowers   after a while
their blooms will die and then
swell into a fruit   and I submit to you   dear viewer
      this process is not monstrous

we've spent too much time

at night watching these shows where the queens
      keep making bad choices
like torching the city with their pet dragons
      or with sickly green fire
            lit in tunnels underneath   because they are mothers
they love their children too much or is it

          not enough   the flowers this spring
are ridiculous   on the way into the theater alone in broad daylight
      for some comic book sequel   I can't stop
shoving my face   into the showy pink organs
      of the parking lot trees

at night I've been balancing like a knife on my side
of the couch   the bed because I'm
too tired already to have anyone really
           touch me

         enough already
with these velvet-eyed children
smudged in ash   cling-wrapped to their mothers' legs   enough
      already with these ruined cities   my children beg
      to come to these movies with me but I declare

         they are not old enough   really I just don't want
      to mediate whose hand is inside whose
   popcorn   whose arm has wandered past
   the neutral zone and into the fraught
territory of someone else's
            armrest   I am wandering

between stories   I keep thinking at night of
              the dinghy waiting outside
the castle wall on tv   if the fallen queen could just
make it there through the rubble   I like to pretend that

        someone would love me enough to arrange
for my escape from the fallen city   even if I've been
a monster   even if I was the one who wrecked it

in the first place and I would dip my oars
          into the sea   and the ripples would scribe
across the water like a message
                              like the little *hi* inscribed

        in ballpoint pen   right at my eye level
on the movie theater bathroom stall where I retreated
          when I had to pee so badly I had to run
                  from the carnage on-screen   how I contemplated

that handwriting   tried to remember
when I stopped wanting to leave behind
          that kind of mark   tried to remember when I was something
          in between the kindling and the torch
                  in there

the brightly lit bathroom   it was clean
          enough   and I didn't have to wipe up
anyone else's pee
          and we all waited nicely
                              with dripping hands
patient for our turn at the dryer

        before opening the door again into the cold darkness
          into whatever reconciliation could be conjured   at the snap
          of the jacked-up hero's fingers   after this

elongated last act   after this interlude

              would my beloved even want
to be stuck in a dinghy with me
          now that I've been crowned the Queen
              of No Fun Anymore   now that I would make
a spreadsheet of who should row

and when   still
with any luck the wind
will discover for us a shore that hasn't even been featured
on-screen
but was mentioned once in passing
by a secondary character   a nice warm place
that the tyrants have forgotten   a shore heavy with blooming

trees and again without permission I would bury my face inside
their bells and hear them ringing out
surrender

and I submit
to you   dear viewer   I cannot fully
remember the many episodes that led us
to this war

The Birds Are Always in the Corn

on the way to see the palace
made of corn and rye and sourdock

I dreamed I was inside it
rearranging the sensibly upholstered
furniture

and you
        not-my-husband
were there in your long wool coat
half-assuring me that you
                            weren't bored

and as always we both kept on
wearing all our clothes   and so I'm still

driving the speed limit along this
                        glistening belt

napping when I have to on gravel roads

off the highway next to the warm
golden grass that waves

over empty silos
                whose aging missiles

the prairie has mostly given up

sunlight floods
        the sparkling ditches and
washed-out roads
                        the towns

I am re-routed from with names
I might have given
                    my daughter

is it too much to ask

Beatrice
           Amelia

why all the flags
           are at half-mast

detoured past slumped sandbags
and houses submerged
               in muddy skirts

I am ashamed to have been so slow

to figure all this beauty   this shining
reservoir trembling the dam

                    constitutes
a disaster

so slow to recall that over and over our buildings
have been wrecked

      to be suspicious of this golden
                    mythic light

suspicious

of such bounty that can mount a palace
made from surplus
          and clad in cob and husk

when will
        the birds descend

and strip its murals bare

         curtain the windows
in their dark feathers
              in a different

      life I would be dreaming
                of unbuttoning your coat

dreaming of the swollen bankless river

down which my empty dress

would float

Wildland-Urban Interface

Today to get ready I used only three beauty tools
that could have set these brittle woods on fire. Then
I painted on my lips. Out the window I thought I glimpsed
a deer with a hunter's head, but the bright orange cap
was just a crown of leaves. The deer are turning up
everywhere. Under rocks. Turning our front door locks.
What's next, antlers tangled up in my old wedding negligee?
At JCPenney years ago when we bought it, my mother worried
it was too sheer. But mother, dear, at that point I had nothing
I would hide. Out my childhood window I dreamed of my body
tucked in buffalo robes and petticoats—wardrobe courtesy
of the pioneer books I'd been assigned—carried in a runner
across the frozen plains. And who was driving?
Out my teenage window I gazed upon herds of bulldozers
instead of bison. Have you seen those photographs, the wall
built from their hunted bones? Please forgive me for
the sprawling neighborhood adjacent to my own: in college
I tongued the man who planned its sewage and running water.
Once he said he liked to imagine me in the bath. I wanted to do
his blueprints in. I missed the prairie. It was complicated. But not
really. I liked being thought of slick and shiny. Pink and perfectly
arranged. Once we met in Vegas where he won a lot of chips,
which he did not split with me. I felt entitled to at least
some portion. He'd ruined my view. My pretend slice
of the wild. Still, we could only pass by the high-stakes tables
where women were tableaus in cocktail dresses. Trophies.
I remember them dripping in furs though that can't be right
because it was so hot outside I thought I'd burst right into flame.
To be blasted with A/C I'd had to duck inside each casino
along the way—The Frontier and Westward Ho, which are
demolished now to make way for slicker towers that don't
even pretend to have heard of the Wild West. Their riprap
tossed into the Las Vegas Wash to stabilize its banks against
the runoff. The wastewater. Whatever we have flushed.
At a steakhouse we ate beneath the eye of a taxidermied elk,
which wasn't really the elk's eye anymore since eyes
are just bags of water that leak or shrink away. So we ate
under glass marbles in sockets that once held the elk's
own eyes, and across the restaurant was a pheasant whose

ring of red feathers was painted on because the real one
soon would fade. Everything I've ever worn has been
someone else's coat. Even the bath is a borrowed skin
of warm and fragrant water.

Dear Highways of Our Nation, I Am Sorry

I did not stop at all of your points of interest. I am sure they were very
interesting. Kind regards. I'm sorry I found your truck stop t-shirts so
stupid I had to get one. Your airbrushed cougars. Thanks again. I'm sorry
I never found the right sign-off for my postcards. With best wishes.
Warmly. The coal cars chugging parallel and then divergent from your
side: somewhere a dark seam is being dismantled and I just watched them
haul it in, haul it in. Fondly. Talk soon. I might complain that the interstates
lack imagination, but they were built when we imagined we'd have to
evacuate our nuclear ruins. Cheers. Ciao. I've lost track by now of how
many gas tanks I've burned right through. Dear highways of our nation,
I'm sorry I did not stop by the cornfields to watch the solstice pour its light
through those half-buried Buicks arranged to mimic Stonehenge. I'm sorry
I drove through your rust-belt cities just to see the fossilized factories. Staged
my bleak photos to leave out all the people. Never spread a blanket on your
shoulder or pulled it off and shook it clean. Sincerely. How have I come so
far yet missed your slow-leaking tanks of drifting mermaids? I want my
heart uncomplicated by their beauty. For that I'd pay and pay. Their hair
made interesting in water. My hand held against the webbing glass. Nothing
funny about it. How long can they keep on swimming. Respectfully. Yours
truly. So long.

"The executioner was very good"

To be queen for a thousand days sounded like
being queen forever   in my childish grasp
of time and math   but my mother told me
one day I'd understand   that a thousand isn't

much   I'd found the books of kings and queens
in her parents' old farmhouse attic   in the boxes
of her old things   to get there we'd driven past
the truck stop   where the huge fiberglass man

loomed out front   Phil   his hands held out
before him as all statues   cast from that mold
right palm up   left hand curled down   ready
to hold a giant version of whatever   muffler or tire

was being sold   in the attic again years later   I read
how rumors gave the queen   an extra finger but when
exhumed she revealed her hands   had always held
the proper number of bones   the king must have

loved her little neck   for he switched out   the blunt
axe for a swifter sharper sword   after my mother's
diagnosis   I googled how many days the cancer would
afford her   because the doctor didn't tell her and she

was too wise to ask   and so I began the countdown
my fingers always ticking down behind her back
until I was left   with just a fist   Big Phil is gone now
from the truck stop corner   a thousand such sculptures

now missing   or in their dissolution repainted   re-
purposed   their props swapped out for other
giant props   a hot dog for a flag   a pitchfork
for an axe   rolled-up carpet for a rifle   stop sign

for an axe   a cutlass for an axe   a giant axe   and she
had *but little neck*   some statues were left in pieces
legs and torsos propped up in junkyards   like an abbey
stripped down into a quarry to re-form less lovely

buildings   the queen was raised upon a scaffold
before she was made to kneel   my mother
in her nightgown was carried   downstairs and out
into the car   like a little paper doll   torn out

from a book   some statues left standing
at the roadside are holding   nothing now   and I
would pile in their arms   the queen's little crimson
kirtle   her unfastened hood   her useless

ermine cloak

Succession

The tapped-out mine outside of town, now superfund,
was named for the owner's daughter. Though
its eight thousand acres run through reservation land,
the tribes there get no claim. My own family
keeps testing our DNA, but my mother's maiden name
means *mud hole*: no crown is hiding in
our tree's branches. Around here one kind
of white noise is the train that keeps rumbling through.
We used to live right by the tracks. Water shook
inside our glasses. When the train slowed,
men hopped off the boxcars to drift into town
through the back alleys by our street. Once
from the kitchen window in early dawn
I saw a stranger trying to balance on my blue bike.
The water glass I had been filling at the faucet
trembled in my hand. In fear or anger? Now
we live up in the hills where the train's sound
rises to us like a tide. The tracks and townsite
were carved out too from what was meant to be
the reservation. The labor performed by those
who never saw the profit. Some of these hills
are ancient, others newly made from the old mine's
overburden. I hoard words like *overburden*. The train
makes huge crashes in its coupling. Like *spoil tip*.
The summits whiten first with snow and then
the land below. I am my father's daughter. By all
measures a good man. As a child I had a special card
that let me on his base. At the commissary
we parked in the spot reserved for Air Force officers.
I made my mother over-tip the baggers. I didn't know
how to act as they loaded up our car. Passenger service
discontinued, it's only freight trains now bearing goods
for other places. In my own vessel I've carried children.
My daughter is old enough now to predict my death.
She's specific, foresees a shipwreck. Her favorite
Disney movie suggests that's how she'll ascend
to queen. Not just yet, she placates me, but when
she's older. She is looking forward. She is testing
limits. The train keeps rumbling through. Water

trembling in my hand. Into the washed-out morning light
years ago I burst outside, hollering for my bike.
During the Cold War my father sat on a runway overseas,
nuclear warhead strapped beneath his wings. Startled,
the poor thief dropped my bike and vanished
in an alley. If he'd been ordered, my father
would have dropped his burden into a cloud.
A bent wheel spinning. How would he return,
my father, from such a mission? I walked my bike
back behind the house and left it leaning there.
I've always been so certain of my shelter.
My father is so gentle. My daughter
sings sweetly in her room where she tries on
a thin blue silky dress encumbered by a train.
She keeps stepping on it. We hear the fabric
rip and rip. I braid her hair into a crown
when she asks me. The train cars slow
but still are clacking. They won't stop here
to reveal their burden. One day I'll set sail
onto a white-capped sea. A throne
is built on missing bodies. A rumbling
rises. See the tree weighed down
by doves? The train cars couple.
Their branches tremble. In a burst,
their wings obliterate the tree.

Afterlife: Proving Grounds

how easily   we are disassembled

         our dummy legs

sticking out from beneath the rubble

and from our hollow chests

         sand

spills out and out   the desert floor split into

         glass

and nothing essential is left   to be uncovered

here   nothing

         like a brain or heart

the city was built just to see how

         it would blow apart

and in our nicest JCPenney clothes

we'd been propped up

         at the window

that otherworldly light

         why did we think

it was one thing

that we were missing   one thing that kept us

from being human   afterward

the inventory   of the blown-through house

         offers up

part after part

         after part

No Season for Figs

May you never bear fruit again. The disciples
heard Him say it. I've been hungry too, told
the car door to fuck off when I bumped my head.
Kicked the dog and shoved my son into his room.
Woe unto. Poor tree. Whose fault, its fruit is born
before its leaves. Then He overturned
the money tables, knocked down the doves
inside their cages. And the blighted tree became
a lesson. Shit. I mean, *Lo.* I could think of a million
better tricks. Why not make some figs appear?
Why not vanquish hunger altogether? The doves,
I forgot they were being sold to be killed
inside the temple. Here, Teacher, a fish
to split. In its empty belly we may find
enough to save us from our anger.

4

Outlook Hazy, Try Again

he was unashamed of crying in Venice,
Rilke wrote, when the gondolier's request to
be granted passage went unanswered in the
fog

> unanswered *as if*
> *in the face of death*

>> because I did not consult the Magic
>> 8 Ball I found lying in the
>> neighbor's ditch today I feel like I'm
>> making a lot of progress

> in my old high school journal I mentioned offhand
> that I had plans to go to the "mental hospital" with
> Angela but I don't remember going to a mental
> hospital or being friends with Angela or why I
> might go to a mental hospital with someone named
> Angela

when Rilke was young his mother
dressed him like a little doll, a
replacement for his dead sister

> *look now*

> always roaming our high school
> halls was our plush mascot mustang
> on two legs

>> do I remember or have I made up
>> that the mascot could only see from
>> one eyehole at a time

> if only what has been lost to
> memory could be restored in
> imagination

> but Angela I'm
>> still drawing a blank

> *look now the moths*

did we ever laugh at the mustang's
wild bucking or was it always sad

today I stashed the overpopulation
of my daughter's stuffed animals in
a warren under her bed

it's a fact in high school I made myself up
into a little confusing doll

the bells that once sounded so clear
to Rilke in the swirling waters now
dragged their sounds like rags

in high school when we broke up
my boyfriend told everyone I was
crazy

the moths have gotten into you

to be fair once I sobbed to him
because on my bookshelf
The City of God was upside down

it just seemed like a sign

look, you were left

I defaced the classics my parents
bought me by darkly underlining
long passages

look

I shook and shook the plastic ball
until the answer I really wanted
rose from the water

I suspected I was missing calls from all
the boys who loved me because a
storm had knocked out all our phones

you were left untouched too long

once I was at Village Inn smoking back when
I smoked and back when you could smoke in
Village Inn and the little boy in the booth

behind me asked his mother if she would
ever die and after she lit a cigarette she said
well that's usually how it goes

                        and that's the kind of answer I
                        might give my kids now

            and now you are shaken

                        today I wept in the dark theater
                        when it became clear the little toys
                        on-screen had been outgrown by
                        their owner

Rilke said that the ungratefulness of
dolls confirms our first suspicion that
we can't be loved
                        all the little moths

            I held my little daughter on my lap
            trying to see past the many layers of
            tulle into which she had carefully
            stuffed herself and oh my god I wept

                        are we not strange creatures,
                        Rilke wrote, for loving *where
                        there is no hope for response*
            look

            and even if I went back and waited
            and waited at Village Inn I'd probably
            never see that mom and son again

                you were left untouched and

                        at high school pep rallies sometimes it seemed
                        like everyone in the auditorium loved the
                        velvet mustang and other times in the
                        auditorium it seemed like everyone loved
                        pelting him with paper they had wadded up

            now you are shaken

I usually roamed in thrift-store rags
through the high school's labyrinth
halls after the tardy bells had sounded

                                   having jettisoned the respectable clothes
                                   picked out for me by my mother

                    the moths have gotten into you

                         so why then do I remember the horse's
                         agreeable stupid face as if it were my own

                    look now
                                        remember searching the plush
                                        pockets and finding only holes
          why do I remember periscoping
          through one eyehole the sweat-
          fogged auditorium

                         the little moths are fluttering

                              what is it rising up from the water

                    all the little
                                   soft animals flooding out from my
                                   daughter's dust-ruffled bed

                    little moths are fluttering

                         what is left untouched in the
                         watery gap between memory and
                         imagination

          look now
                    what is it that I could call to
                    and be granted passage

                         the little moths are fluttering out of you

                              oh Angela please

               show me your face

Orchestra Playing as the Ship Goes Down

It's been diagrammed: First, the ship's stern
rose into the air. Then the liner broke in two
and slipped beneath the water. My college friend
saw the movie thirteen times and belted out the love theme
while we waited in lines for crowded bars.
Over an iceberg she could weep after enough
tequila. My mom had the book from 1955,
A Night to Remember, which was also the slogan
for my senior prom, where my minidress
and combat boots revealed our differing expectations
for my social life. In the movie, the heroine slips
below decks and then climbs back up again
still in her elaborate, waterlogged dress.
My mom's favorite part was when the orchestra
assembled at the grand staircase's top to keep
the first-class passengers calm. Their supposed
final song: her favorite hymn. The book highlighted
the nobler instincts of those aboard. A mother
climbs in bed beside her children and reads to them,
resigned. Yet some waiting below the decks expected
to be saved. My mother, in the story my dad has told,
just turned her face to the side and died. At the hospital,
they'd warned my dad the odds to resuscitate were slim
and at eighty pounds she would be a shipwreck
even if she did: broken sternum and splintered ribs
and no one left at helm. Still I'm grateful he said
go ahead. Some parts of this story I didn't hear
or I've forgotten and I won't ask again. The orchestra
was really playing. Just a different song, a waltz
that when heard across the water from the distance
of a lifeboat could be mistaken for a hymn.

Cold Metal Cup

The squirming cat beneath the tire
revealed that death itself is not
the problem. That awful thump
in our own garage. It happened

once. Often enough. I was a child
and fled to the house's farthest
room to escape his suffering because
I knew nothing could push his parts

back in. Fix him. To be a girl
who could take him twitching
into my lap to ease something inside us.
I will not be given that. I'm not

asking to be immortal. Having
eaten every feast, having heard
already each story where the king
returns again. I do not want

to be eternally in this restaurant
taking for granted the efficiency
of the waitress, the well-known tragedy
of her murdered son. Do not want

to swig and swig from this
copper cup, but to be always
just receiving it, to just now
be noticing the clouds' slow

drift above us. To be given
a room made from more than
memory where the waitress
can return to her son, once again

a teething infant, his dropped
damp plastic beads. A chamber
where I can crawl beside
my mother, touch the skin-warmed

charm still hanging from her neck.
But even in the most distant
tower there's still the rumble
from the garage where your poor

sister killed your cat and you
were in the car and it wasn't her fault
that he was running in stupid
joy to greet us as if we had survived

some ancient shipwreck instead of
just piano lessons for the measly
hour we'd split between us. One day
the old structures will be razed.

Will become a million shining houses
where a million other cats will strut
right through their doors. I can't ask
the waitress to keep bringing me this

same cold metal cup. The waitress
who has always loved my son, too,
when he comes in for fried fish or
minestrone. Again she can't believe

how big he's getting. She gets his name
a little wrong each time. I will
never correct her. There are a
million names to call our sons.

Salvage

What do you know of shipwrecks? This
is Idaho. We are driving around in pickups
big enough to be their own countries. Still,

the disassembled crib in the truck bed looks
like a little splintered ship. All of our friends
with babies have bought their own

slick minimalist cribs. No one wants this old
oak thing with flowers carved like a crown
into its head. In it our children have dreamed,

woke with their legs stuck between the slats,
like figures fastened to a masthead. Could you
imagine yourself a harbor? The kids have so

many dreams, dreams full of lions and islands
made of jelly—they have as many dreams
as they have art projects, and at night

I'm sneaking around the cluttered house shoving it all
into the trash. Once I woke from a dream
with better judgment. I think last night

I dreamed I had nice cursive, but maybe
I'm just thinking of some paperwork
I filled out last week. Once I did dream

I saw my mother, and she said she missed me,
but she was too tall when I embraced her.
Then I dreamed we were going together

to a different country, which was exciting
until I remembered that on the long trip
she'd be miserable, she'd been so chemo-sick,

and then I remembered there is nowhere
we can go together now. The pickup
rudders around back of every thrift shop

where men are tossing useless things
into the dumpsters, and they won't take this
either, and I wonder if anyone else is wondering

if our cargo denotes some tragedy, like
baby shoes never worn, but it's just the kids
are getting older, which I remind myself

is not a tragedy because no child should feel
evicted from a country where they have done
no wrong but to be subject of the king.

Of time. Of shipwrecks, what do you know.
I keep thinking we're leaving some dark thing
behind us, but it is just a fly on the rearview

mirror. When they were babies I couldn't imagine
my children's grown-up faces, but here they are
emerging, inevitable, like sand washing away

from the bones of some long-beached ship.
Tonight in the middle of her big new bed,
my daughter startles awake, tangled

in her sheets. *That did not happen in
our country*, she says to moor herself,
that happened in some imaginary place.

What Now Have You Been Eating

when commanded, she reluctantly spits it
back out
slick and glistening
her mouth
having gleaned the gravel
of its grit

her two-year molars oft packed
with chewed-on chalk

the telltale smudge pasteling her chin

this summer we ripped up
the grass and replaced it
with nothing

this hard drought, our broken
sprinklers

in the temptation of

our dirt backyard no matter
how many rocks she stuffs
into her cheeks

they do not soften into bread
or water

once

when there was nothing to eat
in the desert
we scraped up the earth itself

and were nourished

we believed it was
        commanded

ʔ

the wilting chokecherries drop stone fruit
     unripe
          on the property line

not even they can survive
     this heat

I drag a hose to water deep

to soak down their roots
        to save them

back inside the house
I hear the water grumbling
through the pipes and can't believe

I am allowed to just

     let it spill out
              like this

one day it will run dry   my son

    dreams that in the graveyard
he can't stop his sister from cramming
        tombstones in her mouth

we've had her tested for what minerals
she is missing, what toxic ones
she's taken in   we have to quiz her
hold up modeling clay and paints

do we eat this   *do we eat this*

ʔ

inside this desert once
we planted an oasis   filled
its fountains with water

now inside of this oasis is
                        another desert
        about to break

ʔ

                our backyard
        these stunted junipers
shedding oranging needles

that crackle underfoot when we
try to trace back
                our steps

to a pocket of restful green

                this should be no wilderness

        to be lost in

in the irrigated park across the street
                        we steer clear
of the pebble-sided water fountain
        she likes to lick

ʔ

                and now we have wandered
too far

        into the desert   have broken open
        all the rocks   sucked out all the water

like marrow from a bone   *do we eat*

     this   we demand
of the desert
       swallowing the field

do we eat this   the ocean

devouring the shore   *do we*

  Ꝓ

eat this   her little teeth

are chipped from chewing stone

soon they will fall away and
perfect new ones
     will rise up

by then I dream
spoons of applesauce and soup
will pass smoothly
         through her lips

and behind us the sprinklers
will spray across
everything   even

the glass patio door

our yard greening
over the lines we dug up and then
     buried again

and when I catch a glimpse
of something foreign inside
her mouth

     I will find in there

the entire world

"Touch the mountain that it might smoke"

Socked in by wildfire smoke, we can't see
across the valley, can hardly remember
the mountain that is there. *The veil is thin,*

the religious like to say around here. The night
my mother died, my son crept into my bed.
Talking in his sleep, he said he was speaking

with her, but when I pressed for specifics,
he just pulled the scarf of sleep around himself
tighter. For a while I forgot that happened

and when I remembered I told the story over
and over so I wouldn't lose it all again.
Studies show the memories we recall the most

are the most corrupt, each time remembered
unset from the mold and then reformed.
The purest memories are locked inside

of brains of those who can't recall. I swear
it was into my bedroom's north wall I'd kicked
a hole when I was younger, but see—there's

the patch job beneath the window. I'm not sure
what was inside the wall or if I even looked
or stuck my fingers in, but give me a minute

and I'll come up with something. Give me
a minute and my son will deliver to me
a message instead of breathing deeper

into sleep. Now I remember my hand
on his chest's rise and fall and his bird-thin
sternum and the light was blue in the room

like it was always going to be dawn.

~

This sunset is stupid my son says because
I'd been promising him a good one, the cloudless
skies so white with smoke we couldn't even see

the sun. Isn't that the lighting in the *Inferno*
or did I make that up? Maybe I read a bad
translation. But it is a stupid sunset,

the sky just shrouding from white into
an ashy gray. This smoke comes from
so far away I'm breathing in a loss

I cannot name. Each morning I check
air reports to see if I can let the kids outside.
As if the air inside were pure. This chamber

is not sealed. Something's always drifting in.
This is paradise, Donne said: *there should be
no Cloud nor Sun, no darkness or dazzling,*

but one equal light.

~

Swearing he smells smoke, a lit match, inside
the house my husband paces, pausing every few steps
to sniff. I smell nothing, but he is so insistent
that for a minute I convince myself

I smell it too. But then I have my doubts. Here
I could allude to the disciple who needed
the wound and not just someone else's word for it
and not even just to see it or to touch his hand

upon it but who needed to push his fingers
completely in. Or I could say something
lovely like doubt is woven into the fabric
of belief and is not opposite to it. My son

wants to build the biggest telescope so he can peer
above the veiling clouds and then report back
on the biggest microphone to everyone on Earth, *Yes
everyone, heaven's here,* or *Nope, guys,*

carry on. But don't blame me. For only a second
do I think something has caught flame
in here before dismissing it and moving on
to wilder beliefs like a brain tumor or ghost:

the smoke trying to tell us something like
someone's fallen in a well. And then I remember
all the things I used to burn in my old room,
incense, sage, incriminating notes,

fanning out the smoke through the holes
in the screen that let the screen be a screen
and not just another wall, and am I remembering
it right that no one wanted to believe

that I was setting things on fire?

⸏

When after weeks the smoke finally lifts—not

extinguished, the wildfire, just the wind shifting it
somewhere else—the bright city and the mountain

are sharper than I ever would have guessed.

⸏

She is not so much in this poem because
I too-well remember grief's rocky depths.
But then when I say I will not recall

her face so I can keep it—there it is—
carved down to bone by chemo—costumed
in the full cheeks of childhood in an old

black and white photo—a round scribble
drawn with my fat crayon—it was always
something that I shaped. So give me

her face to ruin. Her face to touch until
it is a smudge, a veil I've worn into a dazzle,
a white-hot ash one breath away from

gasping into flame.

Afterlife: End of Tourist Season

in the dark mountains where we couldn't
see them a group of children

was singing *the bear went over*
the mountain the bear went over and so forth

we dined alone on the restaurant porch

earlier the priest on the staticky radio

said a crowd gathered on the shores
to hear Jesus tell stories

about a man finding treasure
about a man tossing little seeds

what do you mean

we had been the only ones in the museum
of unimportant stuff

considering a chunk of granite that wasn't
a president's face

but just a chunk of granite
blasted from the mountain

what did it mean

it seemed pretty obvious to us

but the dumb disciples made Jesus
explain it and Jesus

was annoyed look we didn't want
to book the hotel's haunted chamber

the room next door was enough

to press our ear against a glass
held to the wall

to hear something shuffling
on the other side

sometimes the folded-up paper
of grief we've been clutching

accordions suddenly out

a ghost or someone changing into
a suitcase-wrinkled dress

but the haunted elevator
only delivered us politely

to our proper floor

the doors opening and still in our fist
a glittering rock

from the mouth of the shuttered mine

what did it mean

we had wanted after all

the doors to open
somewhere else open

upon some vista

and not this familiar
patterned carpet is it

a seed's fault if a bird eats it
or if it is thrown

into a rocky field

a carved-out mountain

and not a meadow
where the children
we couldn't see

were singing and singing

NOTES

"Coliseum" draws on Christopher Woodward's *In Ruins: A Journey through History, Art, and Literature* and incorporates phrases from Alfred, Lord Tennyson's "The Lady of Shalott."

"Afterlife: Abandoned Mall" draws on ideas found in Robert Ginsberg's *The Aesthetics of Ruins*.

"Soliloquy in the Old Nursery" incorporates phrases from J.M. Barrie's *Peter Pan* as well as from William Shakespeare's *King Lear*.

"Field and Glory" adapts a line from Jean Rhys's *Wide Sargasso Sea*: "If you are buried under a flamboyant tree...your soul is lifted up when it flowers. Everyone wants that."

"Thunder has not harmed anyone we know" takes its title from a line in C.D. Wright's poem "Everything Good Between Men and Women."

"The executioner was very good" takes its title from an excerpt of Anne Boleyn's last words on her execution day: "I have heard the executioner was very good, and I have but little neck."

"Afterlife: Proving Grounds" draws on descriptions in Tom Vanderbilt's *Survival City: Adventures Among the Ruins of Atomic America*.

Italicized lines in "Outlook Hazy, Try Again" come from Rainer Maria Rilke's essay "The Unfortunate Fate of Childhood Dolls" and his letter to Mimi Romanelli reprinted in *The Dark Interval: Letters on Loss, Grief, and Transformation*, edited by Ulrich Baer.

"Touch the mountain that it might smoke" takes its title from Psalm 144:5.

Acknowledgments

Many thanks to Greg Nicholl and Susan Goslee for their counsel. To Michael Waters for selecting the manuscript and Ron Mitchell for his editorial attention. Thank you to the College of Arts and Letters at Idaho State University and the Idaho Commission on the Arts for support.

Gratitude to Adam, Reed, and Clara and to my incredibly generous dad and sisters. To my mother, Suzanne, always.

And thank you to the staff and editors of the journals in which these poems first appeared:

Bennington Review:	"O Bird Singing or Whatever"
DIAGRAM:	"Coliseum"
The Gettysburg Review:	"Orchestra Playing as the Ship Goes Down" and "Salvage"
Grist:	"Keepsake"
Image:	"What Now Have You Been Eating"
Narrative:	"Amelia Earhart, Rock Springs, 1931"; "Exodus with Lightly Sleeping Child"; and "Magi"
New Ohio Review:	"Exile Queen"
Nimrod International Journal of Prose and Poetry:	"Afterlife: Abandoned Mall"
Ploughshares:	"No Season for Figs"
Poetry Northwest:	"The executioner was very good"
South Dakota Review:	"Mylar"
Southern Humanities Review:	"Exposure"
Split Rock Review:	"Broken Water Main"
Sugar House Review:	"Afterlife: Formicarium"
Terrain.org:	"The Birds Are Always in the Corn"
Virginia Quarterly Review:	"Blueprint and Ruin"

"Amelia Earhart, Rock Springs, 1931" was reprinted in *Rewilding: Poems for the Environment* (Flexible Press, 2020).

The Michael Waters Poetry Prize was established in 2013 to honor Michael's contributions to *Southern Indiana Review* and American arts and letters.

Previous MWPP Winners

2020—Erin Rodoni

2019—Julia Koets

2018—Chelsea Wagenaar

2017—Marty McConnell

2016—Ruth Awad

2015—Annie Kim

2014—Dennis Hinrichsen & Hannah Faith Notess

2013—Doug Ramspeck

Southern Indiana Review Press